Online Marketing FOR DUMMIES®

SPECIAL EDITION

by John Arnold,
Ian Lurie, Elizabeth Marsten,
Marty Dickinson,
and Michael Becker

WILEY

John Wiley & Sons Canada, Ltd.

Online Marketing For Dummies,® Special Edition

Published by
John Wiley & Sons Canada, Ltd.
6045 Freemont Blvd.
Mississauga, ON L5R 4J3

www.wiley.com

ISBN: 978-0-470-94157-7

Printed in Canada

1 2 3 4 5 PC 14 13 12 11 10

For details on how to create a custom book for your company or organization, or for more information on John Wiley & Sons Canada custom publishing programs, please call 416-646-7992 or email cupubcan@wiley.com**.**

For general information on John Wiley & Sons Canada, Ltd., including all books published by Wiley Publishing Inc., please call our distribution centre at 1-800-567-4797. For reseller information, including discounts and premium sales, please call our sales department at 416-646-7992. For press review copies, author interviews, or other publicity information, please contact our publicity department, Tel. 416-646-4582, Fax 416-236-4448.

WILEY

About the Authors

John Arnold's uncommonly effective Web marketing strategies are featured in popular Web marketing books, syndicated columns, blog articles, and seminars. John is the author of *E-Mail Marketing For Dummies;* and he is an engaging conference speaker, media contributor, and Web marketing consultant.

Ian Lurie started his Internet marketing company, Portent Interactive, in 1995. He is a long-time Internet marketing geek, with a blog, a book, and occasional speaking gigs on the subject. Ian's diverse background includes degrees in history and law; experience as an information designer, graphic designer, marketing copywriter, and programmer; two years working in a bicycle shop; and a brief stint as a political hack.

Elizabeth Marsten is the PPC Manager at Portent Interactive, a full-service Internet marketing agency based in Seattle, WA. She oversees all the pay per click (PPC) operations and staff and is also learning the ropes in affiliate marketing and managing many of the affiliate efforts at Portent Interactive as well.

Marty Dickinson launched his first Web site — MusicMates. com — in 1996 as a hobby. Today, Music Mates is one of the largest musician referral services in the U.S. Marty soon began helping other business owners with their Internet strategies through services, writing, and workshop-style training.

Michael Becker is a leader in the mobile marketing industry, taking on the roles of industry practitioner, industry volunteer, and entrepreneur academic. In addition, Michael is a contributing author to *Mobile Internet For Dummies,* has authored more than 40 articles on mobile marketing, oversees an industry blog, and is pursuing his doctorate on the topic of mobile enhanced customer-managed interactions.

Publisher's Acknowledgments

We're proud of this book; please send us your comments at http://dummies.custhelp.com.

Some of the people who helped bring this book to market include the following:

Acquisitions and Editorial

Acquiring Editor: Robert Hickey

Manager, Custom Publications: Christiane Coté

Production Editor: Pamela Vokey

Copy Editor: Heather Ball

Editorial Assistant: Katie Wolsley

Composition Services

Project Coordinator: Lynsey Stanford

Layout: Samantha Cherolis

Proofreader: Lauren Mandelbaum

John Wiley & Sons Canada, Ltd.

    Bill Zerter, Chief Operating Officer

    Karen Bryan, Vice-President, Publishing Services

    Jennifer Smith, Vice-President and Publisher, Professional & Trade Division

    Alison Maclean, Managing Editor

Publishing and Editorial for Consumer Dummies

    Diane Graves Steele, Vice President and Publisher, Consumer Dummies

    Kristin Ferguson-Wagstaffe, Product Development Director, Consumer Dummies

    Ensley Eikenburg, Associate Publisher, Travel

    Kelly Regan, Editorial Director, Travel

Composition Services

    Debbie Stailey, Director of Composition Services

Table of Contents

Chapter 5: Social Media Marketing...............61

Chapter 6: Ten Tips for Effective Online Marketing ...79

Introduction

If your business, organization, or association needs to reach people who use computers for shopping, browsing the Internet, or interacting with others, you need to market yourself online.

Here are some reasons why.

Successful online marketing requires you to place and maintain your messages on multiple Internet streams because your prospects and customers use those same streams to look for products and services. You don't have to be a technical expert to reap the rewards of online marketing, but you do need to understand how people behave when they fire up their Internet browser, e-mail program, or smartphone; that way, your marketing messages are always top-of-mind when customers are ready to make a purchase.

The wide breadth of topics and easy-to-follow tips make this guide perfect for your business, organization, or association. Keep it on a nearby bookshelf or on your desk so you can reference it often.

How This Book Is Organized

This book is really five minibooks, each covering a topic related to online marketing, along with one helpful list of ten tips to make your online marketing efforts as successful as possible.

The content in each chapter stands alone, so you don't have to read all the chapters in order. Scan through the table of contents to find a single topic to refresh your memory or to get a few ideas before beginning a task. Or you can read an entire chapter to gain understanding and ideas for executing one or more parts of an online marketing campaign.

Here's a sneak peek of what each chapter contains:

- ✔ **Chapter 1 — Online Marketing Essentials:** Start here if you're new to online marketing or are looking for a quick refresher course. This chapter fills you in on the process of successful online marketing and offers helpful suggestions on building a compelling Web site.

- ✔ **Chapter 2 — Search Engine Optimization:** Having a cool Web site is great, but how can people find it? That's where search engine optimization comes in. In this chapter you discover how to help consumers find you.

- ✔ **Chapter 3 — Pay Per Click Advertising:** If search engines aren't putting your site at the top of search results, you can gain a top position through pay per click (PPC) advertising. This chapter explains the PPC basics, helps you craft an effective PPC ad, and offers some tips on managing your PPC budget to get the most for your money.

- ✔ **Chapter 4 — E-Mail Marketing:** Every successful marketing strategy entails cutting through the clutter, and few places are more cluttered than the average consumer's e-mail inbox. This chapter helps you create e-mails that stand out.

- ✔ **Chapter 5 — Social Media Marketing:** The past few years have seen a huge surge in the popularity of social media sites such as Facebook and LinkedIn. These sites offer tremendous opportunities for savvy marketers, but they're not without hazards. Here you can explore how your business or organization can make the most of social media without falling prey to its traps.

- ✔ **Chapter 6 — Ten Tips for Effective Online Marketing:** All *For Dummies* books include a top ten list, and this one is no different. In this chapter, you get a handy list of quick suggestions for running a successful Internet marketing campaign.

Icons Used in This Book

Throughout this book, little pictures are peppered on the left side of the page. Here's a guide to what they mean:

 The Tip icon marks tips (duh!) and shortcuts that you can use to make Web marketing easier.

 The Remember icon marks information that's especially important to know. To siphon off the most important information in each chapter, just skim through the paragraphs marked with this icon.

 The Warning icon tells you to watch out! It marks important information that may save you headaches.

 Information highlighted with this icon points out how a technique or tool works in the real world. We might recount something from our experiences or share something we've seen or heard. Nothing speaks louder than history, so don't skip these nuggets of online marketing in action.

Chapter 1

Online Marketing Essentials

The "Build it, and they will come!" days of the Internet are long gone. With literally billions of Web pages online, according to Google, competition for customers is fierce. Most successful business owners have turned to using multiple outlets to promote their products and services through the Internet. And many have outsourced teams of helpers to implement integrated Internet-marketing campaigns. How can you compete?

This chapter introduces you to the Internet marketing process of today: a step-by-step sequence for using the Internet to its fullest potential for your business. The chapter also offers some helpful advice for ensuring that you build a brand that consumers will remember and trust, and provides you with a checklist of issues to discuss with your Web designer to ensure you get the Web site you want. Finally, we offer an overview of how to get people to your site when it's live.

Understanding the Online Marketing Process

Your Web site is an important component to your success with the Internet, that's true. However, it's not the *only* piece of the pie. Creating your Web site is really only about 5 percent (or maybe even less) of what you need to gain any real Internet presence. Sure, having your Web site appear on search engines is important, too. But, for most companies, search engine presence is only another 5–10 percent of the overall opportunity that awaits you.

Today's entrepreneur finds success by following a step-by-step process to grow and run his company via the Internet. The following sections outline this process for you.

Step 1: Get in control

The success or failure of your Internet marketing strategy determines whether food appears on your table next month and whether your bills get paid. You must control any process that affects your lifestyle. Basic components you should be in control of include

- **Original Web site design files, including images, photos, and logos:** If your designer suddenly changes careers, loses interest in your project, or even dies, having access to originals will allow you to transition easily to another service provider.

- **Web site hosting logins:** Every Web site needs a Web site hosting location where all the files are stored and accessed on the Internet. You should always choose your own hosting company and pay the hosting company directly for that service. Any login usernames and passwords that the hosting company supplies should be in your name and in your control. You might very well provide access to your Web site to helpers such as designers, programmers, and marketers, but the only way you'll be able to change passwords if you want to change helpers is if you are in charge of your hosting account.

✔ **Domain name logins and registrations:** Your domain name is the heart of your Web site. It is the most critical component of all. As the business owner, you *must* own your domain name, have it registered in your name, and have exclusive rights to maintain it. Never let your designer, administrative assistant, or even your mother register your domain name for you. A domain name such as *YourBusinessName*.com is tied to the Web server where your Web site resides. If you decide to change hosting companies, the only way to change where the domain name directs is by logging into your *domain name registrar* (the company where you registered your domain name) and changing the appropriate settings. This is something only you should control.

Step 2: Establish your products and services for sale

If you have a business, you need to deal with money, or you won't be in business for long. Part of the Internet marketing process is identifying what products your market wants, how or whether your competition offers anything similar, and what online methods you will use to transact that sale online and deliver the goods.

Step 3: Communicate your solution

Your future customers will visit your Web site with a problem to solve. And, they're hoping you have the solution! Before launching any traffic-building campaign, ensure that your Web site delivers the highest potential conversion rate.

A *conversion* is the point at which a Web site visitor takes the next desired step with your business: for example, buying a product, subscribing to your newsletter, or picking up the phone to get more information. The percentage of visitors who convert — the *conversion rate* — is one of the most critical numbers to keep track of on a weekly, or even daily, basis.

Step 4: Build traffic to your Web site

After your Web site is converting on a small scale, the next step is to increase visitation. This is where press releases, search engine optimization, articles, and podcasting (to name a few campaigns) come in. Hundreds of methods for driving traffic to a Web site exist. Your job is to research each type of traffic generator and decide which outlets fit your budget and desired speed to market.

Each chapter in this book provides detailed steps toward implementing today's most effective Internet traffic builders. Master those first — such as search engine optimization (Chapter 2), pay per click advertising (Chapter 3), and social media networking (Chapter 5) — and you will naturally graduate to other traffic-building opportunities over time.

Step 5: Become the recognized expert in your field

People buy online from other people whom they know, like, and trust. The Web is a tremendous tool for achieving all three, and in a short time and on a shoestring budget. Through your Web site, you can become the expert by sharing what you know about your industry.

Another essential, and often overlooked or misused, component to becoming a recognized authority in your field involves using e-mail (see Chapter 4).

Step 6: Power-partner with others for exponential sales growth

Also known as a *joint venture, power-partnering* is similar to having an affiliate program but on a much larger level, both financially and personally. The process involves finding one very special person who's of high stature in an industry and convincing that person to recommend your product or service to his very large sphere of influence. The results could mean literally thousands of sales for you.

Branding Your Look

If you read any book on marketing or branding, you will see common examples of the ultimate goal of branding: Xerox "owns" the word *copiers*; McDonald's "owns" *hamburgers*; Levi Strauss "owns" the word *jeans*. What word or phrase does your product or service own or aspire to own?

Branding is a simple concept to understand yet sometimes a painstaking process to implement. Big companies pay marketing firms thousands of dollars to have expert teams produce branding strategies over weeks and months of brainstorming. So, if you've been struggling with your branding for a while, you're not alone.

Defining branding

If you're new to this term, you will find many definitions for the word *branding*. Branding is simply getting prospects and repeat customers to see and remember your product as the only solution to their specific problem or need. Other items might be similar, but nothing on the market is exactly like what you offer. Of course, you accomplish branding by all the things you hear about in formal definitions like creating a logo, establishing corporate identity, product packaging, advertising, bonding with customers, and establishing loyalty.

Every word you write and every image you place on your Web site can help you build visitors' perception of you as a leader of your field. People buy from leaders and innovators, not from followers.

Developing a branded logo

Perhaps one of the most overlooked elements of doing business in general — let alone online — is the importance of having a meaningful logo. Many Internet marketing gurus will tell you not to waste your time or money producing a logo. But, if you are promoting a real company on the Web, a good logo is vital: It communicates a lot about your business to a Web site visitor in a fraction of a second. When people see your logo (or lack of one), they can immediately rate various elements of your business in their minds, maybe even subconsciously. Visitors evaluate your

- ✔ Level of professionalism
- ✔ Ability to create or innovate
- ✔ Enthusiasm for your product
- ✔ Level of traditionalism
- ✔ Attention to detail

Visitors will associate words to your business based on your logo's appearance, such as funny, silly, exciting, desperate, growing, content, or curious. So be careful what you ask your designer to create for you.

Professional designers are your best resource for creating a logo that matches how you want your business to be perceived. Keep in mind that logos take time to conceptualize and create. So be prepared that by the time you approve a logo, you might see several versions, costing several hundred dollars.

The best scenario from a time standpoint is when your Web site designer also creates your logo. That way you don't have to worry about the logo designer getting the right formats to your Web designer and waiting for them to communicate. But, many Web designers do not work with logos and require a logo to be submitted before beginning to work on your Web site.

Completing the Web Site Pre-Flight Checklist

Just as you would want to crunch numbers and run what-if scenarios before launching a new company, you want to put your plan for your Web site design to paper as well. Collect information on these 25 top items when submitting your project scope to a Web site designer for a price quote:

- ✔ Company information, including name, address, phone, and e-mail
- ✔ How long you have been in business

✔ The primary goal of your business (what you sell)

✔ A description of your business in 25 words or less

✔ A list of three groups of people who might benefit from your product or service

✔ Your branding slogan

✔ The main domain name for your Web site (Try `www.aplus.net/domains` to search for available domain names and then register them.)

✔ A list of at least three Web sites you like and what you like about them

✔ A list of at least three Web sites you dislike and what you dislike about them

✔ A list of at least three competing Web sites

✔ A description of your potential customers' demographic profile, which you can find by searching `www.quantcast.com` for a high-traffic Web site related to your target industry

✔ Whether your potential customers are Internet savvy or technically challenged (You learn this by attending seminars or networking events where your target audience is present and talking with them.)

✔ What you would expect if you were one of your potential customers

✔ The goals of your Web site (sell product online, generate leads, and so on)

✔ Whether visitors ever need to print pages from your site

✔ What the top navigation buttons will be

✔ What the left navigation buttons will be

✔ What special features will be displayed in the right navigation area

✔ What should be included in the footer of every page of the Web site

✔ Whether you will supply photos, or whether the designer should include photos in the quote

✔ Whether you will supply content, or whether the designer should include copywriting in the quote

- Whether you will supply a logo, or whether the designer should quote a price for logo creation

- Whether the Web site will require an online shopping cart

- Whether you already have an Internet-capable merchant account

- Whether you'll need an online newsletter signup form on the Web site

If you need help with any of these points, check out related sections earlier in this chapter.

Generating Traffic

Business owners often ask, "How can I get my Web site on top of Google?" When asked why they want to accomplish that goal, they respond, "Because it's free!" Um, not really. Generating traffic of any kind to your Web site is far from free. You either have to spend your own time to attract visitors, pay for visitors directly, or hire helpers to do the work required to get the visitors. You could always follow the detailed steps offered throughout this book on your own, but don't forget that your time has value. *No traffic is totally free.*

Having said that, here are five core categories of traffic on the Web that virtually all businesses can benefit from:

- **Free search:** Although effort and time have a cost, many search engines and directories don't require you to pay a fee to get listed. Google, MSN, Yahoo!, and dmoz are good examples. And, by getting the pages of your Web site visible on those search engines alone, you will have the potential of being in front of more than 80 percent of all search engine and directory traffic. Optimizing your site content can help you appear higher in search engine results, as Chapter 2 explains.

- **Paid search:** With the growth in development of measurement tools (such as Google Analytics, for example), paid search has become an accepted and essential form of promoting any product or service.

✓ **Supplying content:** Just when you think every topic has been covered, new angles and opinions emerge. Supplying content to the Web through blogs, really simple syndication (RSS), press releases, articles, and forums, and the growing surge of content pushing to smartphones are traffic-generating processes that are available for you right now to pursue. Internet users will always search for content. You just have to find out what they're searching for and supply them with unique content.

✓ **Offline efforts:** Don't overlook your opportunities to use offline resources to promote your Web site. More than 900 radio talk shows throughout the United States alone need guest experts every day. Offer a giveaway to listeners every time you're on the radio. Networking events, associations, leads groups, and schools and churches are always looking for interesting speakers to deliver short, 30-minute messages to their audience. Deliver content-rich information and suggest a visit to your Web site for a free download or for more information about your company. And always provide the opportunity for people to join your e-mail list. (Check out Chapter 4 for more about e-mail marketing.)

Joe Sabah has appeared on more than 650 radio talk shows around the U.S., most by never even leaving his home. He produces a handy contact list and program at `www.sabahradioshows.com` for getting on radio talk shows.

✓ **Referrals:** Of course, no visitor is a higher-quality visitor than a referral. Referrals will spend more time on your Web site and are much more likely to buy because they have already reached a certain level of trust in you because of the referral.

Whether referrals come from offline or online, always strive to increase visitors who are referred by someone else.

Chapter 2

Search Engine Optimization

*B*uilding a Web site is pointless if no one can find it, and three-quarters of everything that happens on the Internet starts with a hit on a search engine. Search engines drive the Internet. Ignore them, and you might as well turn away three of every four customers who ask for help.

The good news? A high placement in the search engine ranking pages (SERPs, if you want to feel all geeky) can drive tremendous growth. The bad news? You can't bribe or buy your way to the top. You have to get there by building a site that's attractive to search engines and customers alike.

And that's the art of search engine optimization (SEO). Don't get rattled by the term: SEO isn't a black art. We demystify it so you can see how it's nothing but a series of steps and little things you do to move up in the rankings. This minibook walks you through the steps, getting you started on your way up the search result rankings.

Knowing What Makes a Web Site Relevant

Search engines want to know which Web site is the most important for a particular concept. These concepts are represented by *keywords* or *key phrases. New York hotels, chocolate candy, bicycles,* and *wedding dresses* are all examples of these.

Search engines are hierarchical thinkers. After reading billions of pages of content by using little software programs called *spiders,* search engines determine the relevance of each of those pages for a keyword based on a complex series of rules.

When you go to a search engine and type in keywords (*wedding dresses,* for example), the search engine picks the best matches by looking at the following in hierarchical order:

1. A site's authority on the subject of wedding dresses, as demonstrated by links from other sites about wedding dresses

   Every link from other, relevant sites is a vote for the target site's authority.

2. Whether wedding dresses are the main focus of each site, as demonstrated by site structure

3. Which pages on those sites are most dedicated to wedding dresses

4. Whether those pages are more relevant than all the other pages in the search engine's index

All you have to do is get yourself to the top of each of those pyramids, and you're rich!

Well, maybe it's not *that* simple. Thousands or even millions of other sites are all vying for that same top spot. To really compete, you need to know how Web pages are built and how search engines read them. If you know these two things, you can provide what search engines want: a structure that indicates what a page is really about.

Creating Your SEO Worksheet

SEO can take a long time. Plus, changes you make today might impact your rankings months from now, so you need to keep a record of relevant data and changes you make over time. That way, you can refer back to those changes and better understand what worked and what didn't.

If you're serious about SEO, you're going to need to track a number of different statistics over time, including the following:

- **Traffic from organic search:** Your Web traffic report should show you clicks from unpaid search rankings.

- **Keyword diversity:** The number of keywords or key phrases driving traffic to your Web site. Your Web analytics package will give you this. (*Web analytics* comprises using a traffic report to draw conclusions and adjust your marketing strategy. The most popular analytics tool is Google Analytics, `www.google.com/analytics`.)

- **Incoming links, by search engine:** The number of links reported by Live, Yahoo!, and Google.

- **Indexed pages, by search engine.**

- **Sales/leads/other results from organic search:** If your site has a goal, and your analytics package allows it, record the results you get. Traffic is great. Sales are better.

- **Keyword rankings:** Notice how this is last? That's because *keyword rankings don't matter.*

Keyword rankings don't mean much. Traffic and results do. Although ranking No. 1 for a phrase or two is one way to get those extra visitors, getting 500 top-ten listings for less prominent phrases may get you far more visitors and sales, leads, or whatever else you need. Don't obsess about keyword rankings. Obsess about traffic, keyword diversity, and success.

Record these numbers by month (or by week if you're really obsessive). Whatever you do, don't check them every day — you may lose your mind!

A Crash Course in Keywords

For now, keywords (or key phrases) are the focus of successful SEO. Someday search engines may be able to index and rank sites based on *concepts* — by knowing that cars and autos are the same thing — but until then, you need to make some pretty specific choices.

SEO is a long-term undertaking. You may wait months before you see any results. Choose the right keywords and you can see a nice lift in traffic after all that effort. Choose the wrong keywords and your months of effort won't help your business.

Thinking like your visitors

When you optimize your site for search engines, remember that you are not optimizing for the keywords *you* like or think should be associated with your product or service. You are optimizing for the keywords *potential customers* associate with your product or service.

For example, say you sell salad through the Internet. You've found a miraculous way to keep vegetables crisp and prevent lettuce from wilting, and you ship salad to suburban dwellers everywhere.

You research keywords and find that no one searches for *salad.* They search for *mixed greens* instead. You have a choice to make. You can insist on optimizing for *salad,* because that is what you sell. Or, you can optimize for *mixed greens,* get visitors, and then educate them as to why *salad* is better.

Don't try to shove your own beliefs about your product or service down your customers' throats by picking the keywords *you* think they should use to find you. That never works in marketing, and it really doesn't work in search engine optimization. Understand what your visitors will use to find you. You can educate them as to why you're different, and why they should care, after they arrive on your Web site.

If a customer searches for *bicycles* and clicks a link to your site, she'll expect to see information about bicycles. If you sell cars, don't optimize for *bicycles* and then try to tell folks why cars are better. That just frustrates them. Go with your strengths: Optimize for *cars*.

Understanding the long tail

You never optimize for a single word; you optimize for a keyword and the hundreds or thousands of permutations on that word. So, if you're targeting *broccoli,* you're probably also targeting *cream of broccoli soup, broccoli recipes,* and *broccoli coleslaw.* These *long-tail phrases* — longer niche phrases that don't get as many searches — are the real beauty of search engine optimization. By optimizing for one word or phrase, you get the benefit of improved rankings for many more.

Go back to the *salad* example from the preceding section. You decide to optimize for *mixed greens.* After six months of hard work, you're still stuck on the fourth rankings page for that phrase. But your traffic from organic searches has gone up 300 percent. For these reasons, you're not sure whether you should fire yourself or give yourself a raise.

Taking a look at your traffic report, though, you notice something interesting. Traffic from longer phrases that include the words *mixed greens* has gone up. Phrases such as the following are now major traffic generators:

> *mixed spring greens*
> *mixed greens online*
> *buy mixed greens*
> *mixed greens salads*
> *really great mixed greens*
> *where can I buy mixed greens*

All these phrases are driving traffic to your site. Together, the six phrases drive more traffic than *mixed greens* would have.

Behold, the long tail! By optimizing for one phrase, you really optimized for six longer ones. Even though you didn't move up in the rankings for the target phrase, you did move up for these others, and they brought you traffic.

Long-tail phrases work for two reasons:

- ✔ You can optimize for many of them at once by focusing on one shorter phrase.

- ✔ Searchers who visit your Web site from long-tail phrases are generally better targeted and better customers. If folks come to your Web site from a long-tail search result and you have what they want, they're likely to buy.

So the next time you're sweating bullets, staring at your rankings report, and wondering why you haven't moved up, check your traffic report. The long tail might pay off big.

Finding the Right Tools

Luckily, you don't have to guess to find keywords. You can use some of the great tools available to help you with your initial brainstorming.

Working with the Google AdWords keyword research tool

Google recently updated its keyword research tool to show search volumes. That makes the Google keyword tool the only source for Google keyword search data.

To show search volumes, follow these steps:

1. **Go to** `http://adwords.google.com/select/KeywordToolExternal`**.**

2. **Type in a phrase in the Word or phrase box, click the Search button, and you get a report.**

   The report shows searches performed in the previous month, average monthly search volume over the past 12 months, and advertiser competition in Google AdWords.

3. **Click the Columns button to display a list of optional columns to view.**

   Select any columns that you think may provide you with helpful information.

Don't worry about the cost-related options. They are used for pay per click (PPC) marketing research. See Chapter 3 to find out more.

Note: Google frequently tweaks its tools; don't be surprised if what we describe differs from what you see onscreen.

You have a few other options:

- **You can filter results to remove some keywords.** To do this, click the Filter My Results option and enter keywords you don't want in your list.

- **You can also get keyword ideas based on a Web site's content.** Click Website Content and enter a Web address. Google's tool checks the page and pulls keywords based on the words and phrases on that page. The Website Content option is a great way to get ideas for keywords you hadn't thought of. You can also verify that your page is optimized for the right phrases and check competitors' pages.

Watching the news

People are media driven, so it pays to keep current on TV, radio, and print news. If a relevant story seems to be gaining a lot of ground, work it into your Web site.

Going back to the (now somewhat silly) mixed greens example earlier in this chapter: If you see on the news that Mark Starguy is the movie star who lost 45 pounds on the mixed greens diet, you might want to mention his name here and there. Chances are other folks watching the news will remember the star's name and *diet,* but not *mixed greens.* If you show up for *Mark Starguy diet,* you're set.

Using your brain

All the computers in the world can't match your brain for its ability to manipulate language. Don't rely on keyword tools alone. They will eventually lie to you (or at least tell a small fib): Keyword tools lack your insight into your customers.

They can use only the data they have, and that means some-times they'll miss important subtleties, such as the difference between *auto* (as in *automobile*) and *auto* (as in *automatic*).

Your brain is the last line of defense against keyword paraly-sis. If the tools are showing you keywords that simply make no sense, go with your gut and try a different approach.

Picking Great Keywords

After you decide what tools to use, it helps to know the criteria for choosing a great keyword. You need to judge rel-evance, competition, and value.

Judging keyword relevance

Question whether the keyword you found is really relevant to your business. For example, *mixed greens* could mean mixed greens for salad. It could also mean mixed green paint.

After you choose a keyword, test it by plugging it into a search engine to see what results you get. Make sure that you don't see any equally correct but totally irrelevant meanings creeping into the search results.

No keyword is 100 percent relevant. If more than half of the long-tail phrases using that word are relevant to your busi-ness, though, you probably have a winner.

Comparing competition and search volume

If you're facing 200 million other Web sites that are all vying for the No. 1 spot, you might want to choose a different keyword.

Go to Google, Yahoo!, and Live Search and search for the phrase you've chosen. Look at three competitive factors:

   ✔ **The number of competing sites:** If you find more than 10 million competing pages in the search results, you might be facing an uphill battle.

- ✔ **Where you rank:** If you're already on the second page of the results, you might not care how many sites are competing with you.

- ✔ **Your ability to compete:** If you have a daily newsletter on your site about mixed greens, you might be super-competitive, even if a mob of other sites is trying to beat you. You're adding new, highly relevant content every day, and search engines love that. That steady content growth gives you an advantage.

Always balance competition against search volume. Some terms might be so relevant and offer so many potential visitors that any level of competition is worth it. For example, the phrase *wedding dresses* gets over one million searches per month. It's also one of the most competitive phrases on the Internet. But one million searches makes *wedding dresses* so potentially valuable that, if you have any chance of gaining a front-page ranking for it, you have to try. Other keywords might offer only a tiny trickle of traffic — and thus, very little competition.

Your best strategy is to mix your keyword list and optimize for both of the following:

- ✔ **High-volume, high-competition keywords** that require a long-term effort on your part before you gain any rankings

- ✔ **Low-volume, low-competition keywords** that can produce results sooner (This strategy lets you build traffic sooner while still aiming for the home run phrases later.)

Testing with pay per click

Because a search engine optimization campaign can take months to really affect your business, you may want to test your keywords by using a faster method — pay per click (PPC) marketing.

Because you can start and end a PPC campaign in a matter of minutes, doing so is a great way to get a rough idea of keyword viability.

Variables including budget, ad wording, competition, and landing pages can skew your results. Make sure that you use your head when you review results. Read Chapter 3 to find out how PPC works.

Optimizing for Local Search

If you're a local business, a top local search listing can drive customers faster than any other online marketing technique. A top ranking puts you at the very top of the search results.

Local search optimization isn't difficult. But it *does* require a very sustained effort, around three different factors:

- Listings on the local search engines and the directory sites they reference
- Reviews and bookmarks on those same sites
- Local data on your Web site

Optimizing your local search listings

The first step in local search optimization is making sure that your business is in each major search engine's local search directory. To do so, follow these steps:

1. **Search for your business on Google Places, Yahoo!, and Live Search.**

2. **Make sure you fill out all fields requested by the search engine, including the description and hours.**

3. **Submit your Web site to Yelp.com (`www.yelp.com`), Superpages.com (`www.superpages.com`), Yellowpages.com (`www.yellowpages.com`), and CitySearch.com (`www.citysearch.com`).**

   The major search engines crawl these sites to determine relevance and location. Note that other sites are available, too. These basics will get you started.

4. **Make sure that your business is assigned to the correct category in the local listings.**

Getting reviews and bookmarks

You have the listings; now get some attention. This requires the most sustained effort on your part, because you have to get past customers to review your business. Search engines look at the quantity of reviews and bookmarks as one indicator of relevance. Try these two ideas for getting customers to review and bookmark your Web site:

- Send a polite note to all of your customers or provide them with a coupon or other incentive, inviting them to review your business at Google, Yahoo! or Live Local. The more reviews you get (even if they're not all good), the more easily you'll move up in the local rankings.

- Provide an easy way for folks to bookmark your location on the mapping service of their choice. More bookmarks or saved locations on Google, Yahoo!, or Live Local mean a higher ranking, too. You can link to your local listing and let your visitors take it from there.

Optimizing your site for local search

With all of these steps, don't forget that you can optimize your own site, too. Use the following tips to optimize your Web site for local search:

- **Make sure your physical address is on every page of your Web site.**

- **Put your metro area location in a few title tags on your Web site.**

- **Have a very good contact page, with directions.**

- **Consider geotagging your Web site.** No direct evidence shows that this impacts rankings yet, but it probably will soon. You'll need to read up on the geotagging of meta tags, which at the time of this writing still isn't a finalized standard.

- **Get links from other local sites.** Join your local Chamber of Commerce, for example, and get a link from its Web site.

Chapter 3

Pay Per Click Advertising

*P*ay per click is a great way to get a spot for your Web site on the front page of search results and to get in front of people who are specifically looking for what you offer. If you're working on organic search engine rankings but just aren't there yet, pay per click is one resource you should consider using for getting your message to an interested audience.

Pay per click advertising can be a very complex — yet simple — medium to conquer. The concept itself is simple. You post an ad, someone clicks it, and you pay a fee for every time someone clicks. Where it gets complex is in the management of those ads, keywords, and budgeting. This chapter walks you through the most necessary concepts that you need to know to have a successful pay per click account.

Understanding Pay Per Click Advertising

Pay per click (PPC) — also known as *cost per click (CPC)* — is a type of paid advertising, such as paid search, sponsored listings, sponsored links, and partner ads. In a PPC model, the advertiser pays the site that hosts the ad space only if a user clicks its ads and goes through to the *destination URL* or *landing page* — the location on the Internet where the person who clicked the ad ends up.

PPC ads are often used in search engines like Google, Yahoo!, and MSN, generally along the top and right sides of the pages that contain search results. These ads don't appear unless someone performs a search in that engine, and the ads that *do* appear are those that the engine deems most relevant to the user's search results. This way, someone who searches for a baseball glove isn't shown ads for shoes.

Cutting to the Front of the Search Result Line through PPC

PPC advertising has evolved as a way for companies, people, and sites to purchase a spot on the first page of search results. Often, the first result page has room for only about ten results, and few people click to see what's on page 2, 3, or beyond. So if your site has low *natural search rankings* (where your Web site appears in the search results), PPC is a way to buy a spot in front of the most people.

Suppose that your law firm practices landlord–tenant law, but your Web site is pretty outdated, and you haven't done any search engine optimization updates (see Chapter 2 for more on SEO). When a user searches for, say, *landlord tenant lawyer* or *landlord law firm*, your firm's Web site is on page 10 of the search results.

That page is buried pretty far back, so the chances are low of getting noticed by people who are specifically searching for your type of law firm. Often, instead of going through the search results page by page, searchers change their search terms and try again. In this case, your firm stays buried. So how do new clients find you?

Certainly, you want to work on your SEO, but that project takes time — not only to research what to do, but also to implement and wait for the results. In the meantime, you can buy yourself a spot on that first page of results and be seen by people who are looking for the service you provide. For this example, your law firm can even create *geotargeted campaigns* (marketing campaigns that focus on a selected market area) that show your ads only to people in the geographic region that your law firm serves. Whether that region is a metropolitan area or an entire state, PPC gets your firm's name directly in front of people who are already interested in what you do.

Considering Other Benefits of PPC

Trying out PPC advertising has many benefits:

- ✔ It's advertising that anyone can do.

- ✔ It gives advertisers a lot of control over their budgets and audiences.

- ✔ It has a great amount of accountability in terms of where the sale occurred, how much it cost, and which keyword and ad triggered the sale.

If PPC advertising is done correctly, the results can be measured very accurately to give the advertiser an idea of what the next steps should be.

Getting measurable results

PPC not only allows you to purchase a spot in front of potential clients or customers, but it also allows you to test things quickly. If you're redesigning an outdated site but aren't sure which version of the Contact Us page you want to use, for example, you could set your campaign to send half of your visitors to one page and half to another page. Then you can measure the response in easily interpretable results, such as these:

- ✔ What keywords did people use to find your site?
- ✔ How many people filled out the form on a landing page?
- ✔ How many people called the firm directly?
- ✔ How many people left the site after visiting the landing page?

With PPC, you can drive visitors to your pages quickly and often, rather than wait for visitors to appear naturally.

Spending your money wisely

PPC enables you to set daily budgets for an account or campaign and edit bids on a per-keyword basis. (Go to the end of this chapter for more about bidding on keywords.) If you're trying to determine which keywords to target for search engine optimization purposes (as we discuss in Chapter 2), you can use PPC to measure the success and popularity of those keywords and, at the same time, limit how much you spend on that experiment. You can also set your budget to spend by time of day or geographic region and even turn your ads off, either automatically or manually. PPC gives you a lot of flexibility for managing both the cost and the frequency of your ads.

Finding niches

Particularly if your company is in a highly competitive market, you can use PPC to find a niche that isn't as competitive as others or that you can specialize in. Searchers give you a lot of information when they come to your site: what keywords brought them there, what pages they visited, how quickly they left, and what they bought or downloaded. To return to the law firm example, if you find that you're receiving conversions from the keyword phrase *lawyers for landlords,* you can build a specific ad group and ad around that keyword to target searches better — and at a lower cost to you.

Determining Which Keywords to Use

The *keyword list* is the foundation on which your campaigns are built. A good, well-organized keyword list can make a lot of difference in how your account performs — or doesn't perform.

Generate keywords that describe your product or service, such as colors, styles, sizes, or brands. Depending on how popular these terms are, they might have to be sectioned off into separate ad groups or campaigns.

Also, if you sell a variety of products, you want to have a separate ad group for each product you promote.

Suppose that you sell two different types of pens: ballpoint and gel. Also suppose that you want to promote six kinds of ballpoint pens but only one type of gel pen. Putting the keywords for the gel pen in with those for the ballpoint pens may save you a little time, because you don't have to create a separate ad group for the gel pen, but overall, combining these keywords won't produce your desired PPC result or return on investment.

For the same reason, you wouldn't bid on the keyword *pen* in either ad group. The term is too general and *high traffic* (a very popular term likely to generate a lot of impressions and clicks), and it isn't as targeted as *ballpoint pen* or *gel pen.* A high-traffic keyword like *pen* may need to be in its own campaign because it's so broad that it will generate a lot of traffic, much of which could have nothing to do with your pen. Your ad could show up for totally unrelated inquiries such as *pig pen, pen pal, pent up,* and *penny,* for example.

The best practice is to decide the subject of your campaign before you select keywords. Sketch out your subject and keep it in mind while you're building your ad groups and keyword lists.

Organizing Keywords in Ad Groups

Organizing your keywords in ad groups makes managing your campaigns easier and cleaner, and shows much more clearly which keywords are successful and which ones aren't. In this section, we give several examples of just how thoughtful you need to be when you organize your keywords in ad groups.

Suppose that you sell floral wedding invitations. You want to promote the type/brand Flora Wedding Invitations, and you know that rose, lily, and daisy invitations are very popular. To plan your campaign, you might create a table like Table 3-1.

Table 3-1	Ad Groups and Keywords for a Sample Campaign
Ad Group	**Keywords**
General Floral Wedding Invitations	*flower wedding invitations, floral wedding invitations, flower wedding invites, floral wedding invites*
Rose Wedding Invitations	*rose wedding invitations, rose wedding invites, pink rose wedding invitations, pink rose wedding invites, red rose wedding invitations, red rose wedding invites*

Ad Group	Keywords
Lily Wedding Invitations	*lily wedding invitations, lily wedding invites, calla lily wedding invitations, calla lily wedding invites*
Daisy Wedding Invitations	*daisy wedding invitations, daisy wedding invites, yellow daisy wedding invitations, yellow daisy invites, gerber daisy wedding invitations, gerber daisy wedding invites*
Flora Wedding Invitation Branded	*flora wedding invitations, flora wedding invites, flora company wedding invitations, wedding invitations flora*

From the start, make your keyword lists as segmented and relevant as possible. Although cramming everything into a few ad groups may seem like less work, that practice will actually create more work and headaches for you down the line as the account matures.

The example in Table 3-1 is a highly segmented campaign of several ad groups and keywords. Even though the ad groups are highly targeted, they're within the same campaign which will give you greater control of cost and allow you to add *negative keywords* (keywords you don't want your ads to appear in conjunction with) easily.

Creating an Attention-Grabbing PPC Ad

Ad copy is a two-second chance to catch a searcher's attention, so clearly your ads need to quickly grab and then keep a reader's attention. A PPC ad is made up of the following elements:

- ✔ Headline
- ✔ Body
- ✔ Display URL
- ✔ Destination URL

Of the four elements in a PPC ad, your headline is the most important part. Most often, searchers don't read whole ads; they scan the headlines to narrow down their choices. Keeping this fact in mind, the best practice for any PPC ad is to use a high-traffic keyword (your most revenue-generating one, if possible) in the headline.

A *revenue-generating keyword* is one that you know brings in results, whether those results are sales, downloads, or signups. A *high-traffic keyword* is one that drives a lot of impressions and clicks but doesn't necessarily result in sales. Some campaigns have a keyword that meets both those criteria. Check your analytics package, if you have one (and if you don't, you should — refer to Chapter 2), or check the past performance of that keyword in the PPC interface to determine what your high-traffic and revenue-generating keywords are.

If the keyword you want to use is a longer, more targeted word, simply using the keyword alone as the headline (depending on length) is all you need to do to capture a searcher's attention. Typically, search engines limit a headline to 35 characters, although Yahoo! Search Marketing allows 40 characters.

Determining Your PPC Budget

The most important aspect of your PPC account is money. The amount you spend and how you spend it determine the overall outcome of your campaigns — unless, of course, you have an unlimited budget and don't need to see a positive return on your investment. Very few marketers fall within that category, though.

The very first question you should ask yourself is "How much can I spend?" After you establish how much you can spend, you can really expand and optimize your account.

Setting your expectations

Establish your PPC marketing budget with the assumption that you might not make it all back. Any get-rich-quick promises or pitches that guarantee that you'll quadruple your return on investment are just as fishy as they sound. Not all industries, products, or services flourish in PPC. Industries that sell equipment retailing for thousands of dollars might have a much harder time than a site that sells shoes, for example. Those types of industries should consider PPC to be a tool for gathering leads for sales and increasing brand awareness. Building your campaigns smartly and capping the amount you spend per day with careful budgeting ensures that you get the most bang for your buck.

Sticking to your budget

After you figure out how much you can spend, stick to that number. PPC is a little like gambling; you shouldn't assume that you're going to "win" big every time. Determine what you can spend, assume that you won't make your investment back — and don't dip into your savings to spend more money than you initially budgeted! If what you tried didn't work and you want to try again, change your account through optimization techniques (refer to Chapter 2) before spending more money.

Bidding on Keywords

One of the most complex aspects of PPC management is bid management. Most search engines require you to set your bids when you set up an ad group.

Bids are set at two levels:

- **Ad-group level:** At ad-group level, you must set a maximum bid — the largest amount that you're willing to pay for a single click. You may not pay that actual amount, but be prepared to do so.

- **Keyword level:** A keyword-level bid is the maximum cost per click (CPC) you're willing to pay for that single keyword.

  By default, all keywords receive the ad group's maximum CPC.

Knowing how CPC is determined

Search engines determine cost per click (CPC) based on their own algorithms. These algorithms calculate various factors to determine the minimum bid for a given keyword, the smallest amount that the search engine will charge for that keyword, and the rate you pay for it.

Search engines keep their algorithms as closely guarded secrets so that advertisers can't exploit or cheat the system. Google, Yahoo!, and MSN, however, use several known factors to calculate CPC:

- Relevancy of the keyword to your ad

- Relevancy of the search term to your keyword

- Destination URL (where the ad takes the searcher)

- Daily budget

- Keyword bid amount

- Amount of competition

- Relevancy of the competitors for that keyword compared with you

Deciding what to bid

When you select your keywords or use keyword tools to add new ones, most search engines show you an estimated number of searches, CPC, and cost per day for each keyword. Those estimates are valuable tools for determining your maximum CPC.

A best practice in setting a maximum bid for an ad group is to start high and lower that bid as necessary. This practice gives you a running start with the search engine. Your ad will appear quickly and often, giving you results much sooner than if you start low and try to work your way up. This technique also places your ads in good positions on the result page; a higher position on the page means increased visibility to searchers.

Chapter 4

E-Mail Marketing

E-mail marketing represents an opportunity to experience both the thrill of increased customer loyalty and steady repeat business as well as the agony of bounced e-mail, unsubscribe requests, and spam complaints. But whether you find thrill or agony depends on your ability to effectively deliver valuable and purposeful e-mails to prospects and customers who need your information.

This chapter combines time-tested marketing strategies with consumer preferences and best practices to help you develop and deliver professional-looking e-mails that your prospects and customers will look forward to receiving. Additionally, this chapter shows you how to turn your prospects into loyal customers who buy more.

Understanding the Benefits of E-Mail Marketing

E-mail might seem like a cost-effective way to deliver your marketing messages. For the most part, it is, because you can send personalized, targeted, and interest-specific messages to a large number of people. The value of e-mail marketing doesn't end with the cost, however. E-mail marketing has certain advantages over other forms of direct marketing, both for your business and for the people who request and receive your e-mails.

Asking for immediate action

You don't have to wait around too long to determine whether an e-mail message was successful. According to MarketingSherpa (www.marketingsherpa.com) *Email Marketing Benchmark Guide 2007*, 80 percent of the e-mail you send is opened in the first 48 hours after delivery.

After an e-mail is opened, your audience can take immediate action because taking action involves one click of the mouse. Immediate actions include

- ✔ Opening and reading the e-mail
- ✔ Clicking a link
- ✔ Clicking the Reply button
- ✔ Forwarding the e-mail
- ✔ Printing the e-mail
- ✔ Saving the e-mail

Gathering feedback

E-mail is a two-way form of communication, and even commercial e-mail can be used to gather feedback and responses from your audience. Replying to e-mails is simple, and many consumers love to share their opinions when doing so is easy. Feedback from e-mails comes in two basic categories:

✔ **Stated feedback** happens when someone

- Fills out an online form

- Fills out an online survey

- Sends a reply

✔ **Behavioral feedback** happens when you track

- Link clicks

- E-mail open rates

- E-mails forwarded to friends

Generating awareness

When was the last time you mailed thousands of postcards, and your customers began crowding around photocopiers to duplicate the postcards, stick stamps on them, and forward them to their friends? E-mail programs have a Forward button so users can easily send a copy of your e-mail to one or more people. *E-mail service providers* (ESPs) also provide a trackable Forward link that you can insert into your e-mails to find out who is forwarding them. To find out more about ESPs, flip ahead to the section "Taking Advantage of E-Mail Service Providers" later in this chapter.

Staying top-of-mind

If you send out periodic e-mails with valuable content, people who aren't ready to buy right away are more likely to remember you and your business when they become ready to buy.

Combining E-Mail with Other Media

In marketing, you're likely to use several media and messages to communicate everything necessary to attract and keep customers.

Delivering your messages by combining different media is an effective way to market your business, but you'll probably find it more affordable to lean heavily on a few communication media that give you the highest return. E-mail is one such medium because it's cost-effective and the returns are generally outstanding.

Keeping the design elements and personality of your e-mails and other messages similar or identical over time — *branding* — reinforces each of your messages and makes each successive message more memorable to your audience.

Consumers are more likely to respond positively to your e-mails when they can identify your brand and when the content of each message feels familiar. Plan all your marketing messages as if they were one unit to ensure they all contain design elements that become familiar to your audience.

Here are some branding ideas to help you give all your marketing messages a familiar look and feel:

- **Make your logo identifiable and readable in all types of print and digital formats, with color schemes that look good online and in print.**

  In general, your logo and colors should look consistent on

  - Signs

  - Order forms

  - E-mail signup forms

  - Your Web site

  - Receipts

  - Business cards

  - E-mails

- **Include your company name in all your marketing.**

  Incorporate your name in

  - E-mail From lines

  - E-mail addresses

- Your e-mail signature

- Online directories

- Your blog

✔ **Format your messages consistently across media.**

When repeating messages in multiple media, make sure the following elements are formatted consistently in your e-mails:

- Fonts

- Layouts

- Images

- Headlines

- Contact information

- Calls to action

Sending commercial e-mail to complete strangers is illegal. To keep on the right side of the law, initiate contact with prospective customers through a medium other than e-mail. For more about the legality of sending commercial e-mail, see the section, "Becoming a Trusted E-Mail Sender," later in this chapter.

Taking Advantage of E-Mail Service Providers

The days when you could send a single e-mail and *blind-copy* hundreds of other people — by adding e-mail addresses to the message's BCC field — are over. Spam filters, firewalls, junk folders, and consumer distrust are all reasons to turn to professionals for help with your e-mail strategy. *E-mail service providers (ESPs)* are companies that provide one or more of the following commercial e-mail services:

✔ Improved e-mail deliverability

✔ Database and list management

✔ E-mail template design

- E-mail message and content creation
- Tracking reports
- Advice and consulting

Exploring provider benefits

ESPs let you do much more with your e-mail marketing than you could on your own. Some ESPs even provide various levels of outsourcing for higher prices if you don't want to do your own e-mail marketing. Here are a few examples of the benefits ESPs provide:

- **Give your business a professional look.** ESPs can help you create great-looking e-mail communications without programming knowledge. Most ESPs provide templates with consumer-friendly layouts to accommodate any type of message. Some ESPs provide template-creation wizards so you control all your own design elements for a low cost, and some ESPs either include professional services to help you with semi-custom designs or allow you to completely outsource and customize your template designs. Here are some of the templates that ESPs usually provide:

  - Newsletters

  - Promotions

  - Announcements

  - Press releases

  - Event invitations

  - Greeting cards

  - Business letterhead

- **Keep your marketing legal.** ESPs are required to incorporate current e-mail laws for customers to easily comply. Reputable ESPs take compliance a step further than the basic legal requirements and adhere to more professional standards that reflect consumer preferences. Examples of professional standards include the following:

  - Safe one-click unsubscribe links

  - Privacy statements

- Physical address added to e-mails

- Sending from a verified e-mail address

✔ **Help you with logistics and reporting.** ESPs can help you manage the data and feedback associated with executing your e-mail strategy. Here are some ways ESPs manage your information:

- Store and retrieve subscriber information

- Report on deliverability

- Handle subscribe and unsubscribe requests automatically

- Track information on blocked and bounced e-mail

✔ **Help with content.** ESPs want you to be successful because if your e-mail messages are effective, you'll likely reward your ESP by being a loyal customer. Many ESPs have resources that will help you develop your content and use best practices. Examples include

- Online communities

- Webinars

- Tutorials

- Classroom-style training

- Consultation

✔ **Teach you best practices.** ESPs can give you valuable information on consumer preferences and professional standards that would be too expensive or impossible for you to obtain on your own. ESPs send a lot of e-mails for their customers, so they really know their stuff. Some ESPs are willing to share their knowledge to make your e-mails more effective. Some things you might find out include

- Best times and days to send

- How to improve your open rates

- How to avoid spam complaints

- What to do when e-mail is blocked or filtered

- How to design and lay out your content

Becoming a Trusted E-Mail Sender

Every e-mail marketing strategy is subject to the possibility of consumer spam complaints, and numerous legal and professional standards apply to commercial e-mail. Consumers also expect marketing e-mails to come from a trusted source with just the right frequency and amount of content.

Adhering to e-mail professionalism keeps your e-mails legally compliant and improves your relationships with the people who receive and open your e-mails.

This section is intended to broaden your understanding of industry practices and shouldn't be used to make decisions regarding your own compliance to the law. Contact your lawyer if you need more information.

Collecting e-mail addresses legally

Make sure that you have explicit permission from everyone on your list to send them e-mail. Here are some best practices for steering clear of potentially permission-less e-mail addresses:

- ✔ **Never purchase an e-mail list from a company that allows you to keep the e-mail addresses as a data file.** E-mail addresses kept in a data file are easily bought and sold, and e-mail addresses with explicit permission are too valuable to sell.

- ✔ **Never collect e-mail addresses from Web sites and other online directories.** We advise against this practice because you don't have affirmative consent (or permission) from the owner.

- ✔ **Don't use an e-mail address collection service.** The exception is a service that collects confirmed permission from every subscriber that it obtains.

✔ **Don't borrow an e-mail list from another business and send e-mail to that business's e-mail list.** Those subscribers didn't explicitly opt-in to receive your e-mails.

✔ **Don't rent an e-mail list unless you're certain that the list rental company's practices are legally compliant.** Most rental companies don't have permission-based lists.

Including required content in your e-mails

In the U.S., lawmakers enacted the CAN-SPAM (Controlling the Assault of Non-Solicited Pornography and Marketing) Act of 2003 to help prosecute spammers. (Unfortunately, Canada has yet to adopt anti-spam laws, although new legislation is currently in the works.) The CAN-SPAM Act requires you to include certain content in your e-mails. Include the following in your e-mails to stay CAN-SPAM compliant:

✔ **Provide a way for your subscribers to opt-out of receiving future e-mails.**

You're required to permanently remove anyone who unsubscribes from your e-mail list within ten days of the unsubscribe request, and you can't add that person back without his explicit permission. When providing an opt-out mechanism, remember that it's illegal to charge someone to opt-out or to ask for any information other than an e-mail address and opt-out preferences. You must allow subscribers to opt out by replying to a single e-mail or by visiting a single Web page. Your ESP can provide you with an opt-out link that automatically unsubscribes in one click.

✔ **Make sure that your e-mail includes your physical address.**

If your business has multiple locations, include your main address or the physical address associated with each e-mail you send.

If you work from home and don't want your home address in every e-mail, the CAN-SPAM 2008 revisions confirm that you're allowed to include your post office box address as long as the post office or box rental company associates the box to your legitimate business address.

- ✔ **Make sure that your e-mail header information clearly identifies your business and isn't misleading to your audience in any way.**

  Your e-mail header includes your From line, Subject line, and e-mail address. Make sure all this information clearly and honestly represents your business. The term *misleading* is open to legal interpretation. Speak to your attorney if you have questions.

- ✔ **Make sure that your e-mail's Subject line isn't misleading.**

  Don't use the Subject line to trick your audience into opening your e-mail or to misrepresent the offer contained in your message.

- ✔ **Make sure that your e-mail clearly states that it is a solicitation.**

  The exception is when you have permission or affirmative consent from every individual on your list to send the solicitation. (Read more about permission later in this chapter.)

Collecting Contact Information

The quality of your e-mail list depends greatly on where and how you collect the information in the first place as well as where and how you store and manage the data. Obtaining information and permission directly from the people who own the information — namely, your prospects and customers — is the best way to build a quality e-mail list.

Your challenge is to provide multiple opportunities and incentives for prospects and customers to share their information. You must then manage the resulting data effectively and efficiently.

Deciding what information to collect

The two things you need to collect are an e-mail address and permission to send someone a professional e-mail. Generally speaking, enlisting subscribers is easier if you ask for as little information as possible. You'll improve your results in the long run, however, if you make plans to gather more information over time — such as interests and personal information — as you interact with customers and prospects.

Table 4-1 lists several types of information you can ask prospective e-mail list subscribers for to help you build a valuable list.

Table 4-1	E-Mail List Information Collection		
Category	*Description*	*Use*	*Examples Include*
Essential Information	Information that your customers or prospects expect you to know	Use to personalize your e-mails	Preferred e-mail address First name ZIP code
Behavioral Information	Indicates how your audience is likely to act toward your e-mail content	Use privately to group your list subscribers into categories for targeted messages	Prospects Coupon users Repeat purchasers Advocates Very Important Customers (VICs)
Personal Information	Reveals important details about the person you're sending to	Use to send more relevant information	Gender Marital status Family info Preferences

You don't have to obtain all subscriber information the first time you contact a prospect or customer. As long as you have a good permission-based e-mail address, you can ask for more information in future e-mails by

- Sending short, relevant e-mail surveys

- Asking for information in the context of your regular e-mails

- Using forms and links on your Web site to collect information from people who are browsing or buying

- Asking for more information through other marketing media as more trust develops in your relationship

---

When is essential information essential?

How your prospects and customers view essential information is likely to depend upon how personally you interact with them at the beginning of the relationship. People are also more comfortable sharing information when they understand how you'll use it.

For example, an online retailer could be viewed as intruding when asking a site visitor for a physical address before he's ready to make a purchase. After the site visitor decides to check out with an item in the shopping cart, collecting a physical address becomes necessary to ship the item.

Collecting information through print

Adding signup information to direct mail and print advertising is a great way to help maximize your advertising dollars. You can use print to drive people to your Web site or store, you can ask them to fill out a paper form and return it, or you can ask them to send you an e-mail requesting to join the list.

Here are some ideas for using print to drive people to a signup process:

- **Send a postcard offering an incentive to return the card to the store (such as a free gift or an entry into a draw) with the recipient's e-mail address filled into a space on the card.** Be sure to explain how you intend to use the e-mail address and ask permission in the text.

- **Position your signup incentive to add value to your print offer.** For example, you could print

  Free child's haircut with subscription to our preferred customer e-mail list.

- **Add your signup incentive to the back of your business cards.** For example, a discount store's business card could include

  Our e-mail list members save 10% more! Join online, in person, or by phone.

✔ **Purchase an intuitive domain name and place it in your print advertising to promote signups.** In the preceding example, the discount store could purchase a domain such as www.JoinMyEmailList.com, and point it to the signup form on the company Web site.

Offering Incentives to Increase Signups

Because your e-mail list is an asset — hopefully containing the e-mail addresses of loyal customers who spend more money as well as referral sources who love to tell others about you — offering an incentive in exchange for an e-mail subscription is really the least you can do to thank and reward your most valuable contacts.

Offering incentives for joining your e-mail list can reward your business in at least two ways:

✔ **Increased signups:** The number of people willing to share their contact information with you is likely to increase if they feel that they're getting something of value in return.

✔ **Increased loyalty:** An incentive rewards your subscribers, who may give you more loyalty, repeat business, and referrals.

Preparing Your E-Mail Database

After you collect e-mail addresses, you need to store your list data in a useful electronic format so that you can send out e-mails easily, so take care to enter your data into a database as you collect it. Building and maintaining an electronic database allows you to

✔ **Organize and view your list data easily.**

✔ **Sort your list data into categories to send targeted e-mails.** For example, you might use your database to sort your data by ZIP or postal code so you can send a more targeted event invitation to people in a specific region.

> ✔ **Process and keep track of unsubscribed contacts.**
>
> ✔ **Query your list to extract useful information and reports.**

Branding Your E-Mails to Enhance Your Image

As we discuss in Chapter 1, *branding* means using graphic design elements to give your business a consistent and unique identity and form a mental image of your business's personality. Examples include

> ✔ Graphics and logos unique to your business
>
> ✔ Text and fonts that differentiate your business
>
> ✔ Colors used consistently to give your business an identity

Branding your e-mails helps your audience to immediately recognize and differentiate your e-mails from the unfamiliar ones they receive. Keeping your branding consistent allows your audience to become familiar with you and your e-mails over time.

Branding your e-mails with colors and design elements requires using HTML. If you don't know HTML, look to your e-mail service provider (ESP). Most ESPs allow you to customize your e-mail templates with your branding elements. If you aren't using an ESP to send your e-mails, a Web designer can help you create templates with a custom look and feel.

Matching every e-mail to your brand gives your audience confidence. It also makes your business more memorable every time your audience clicks to access your Web site or walks into your store and sees the same branding elements.

You can design your e-mails to match your brand in the following ways:

> ✔ **Include your logo in your e-mails.**
>
> Position your logo in the upper left or top center of your e-mail where readers are most likely to see it.

Using a company logo along with identifiable design elements brands your e-mail and reinforces your company's image.

✔ **Use the colors from your logo in your e-mails.**

If your logo has multiple colors, pull the colors from your logo and use them for the borders, backgrounds, and fonts in your e-mails. If your logo uses only one color, you can use a graphic design program to create a palette of colors that work well with the color in your logo. You can find a list of helpful color-matching tools at `www.easycontact.com`.

✔ **Use the colors from your Web site in your e-mails.**

When readers click from your e-mail to your Web site, they might hesitate if your Web site looks different from your e-mail. When you design your e-mails, use the colors in your Web site in a similar fashion. For example, if your Web site uses a gray background with black text, use the same colors for those elements in your e-mails.

✔ **Match your Web site offers with your e-mail offers.**

If your e-mail includes an offer with a specific design, make sure that your Web site uses the same design elements in the offer if you're directing people to your Web site to buy something or to read more about the offer.

✔ **Match your print communications to your e-mails.**

If you're sending direct mail or printing ads to follow up or reinforce your e-mails, make sure that your print communications match your e-mails and the rest of your communications.

✔ **Use fonts that match your brand in your e-mails.**

Consistent fonts add to the overall look and feel of your e-mails. They also add emotion behind the text. Keep your fonts consistent in all your communications and use the same fonts for similar visual anchors. For example, if your e-mail contains three articles with three headlines in one column, use the same font for each headline in the column. Just don't use too many different kinds of fonts in one e-mail. Stick with two or three fonts to avoid heaping visual distractions on your audience.

> ✔ **Make sure your e-mails reflect your business's personality.**
>
> Just as you want design elements that match your brand, your writing should match your business's personality, too. Show your e-mails to a few trustworthy friends or advisors and ask them to tell you whether your writing style matches your image. If you aren't a good writer, consider using a copywriter to help you maintain your image using the text of your articles and offers. Tell your copywriter whether you want the text in your e-mail to make your business seem
>
> - Serious or humorous
>
> - Professional or casual
>
> - Formal or friendly
>
> - Exclusive or universal
>
> - Urgent or customary
>
> - Insistent or politely persuasive

Here are some ways you can brand multiple e-mail formats with consistency while giving each format a unique identity:

✔ Use the same top-bar image with slightly different colors for each format.

✔ Change the colors in your logo slightly for each format.

✔ Use slightly different colors for backgrounds and borders in each format.

✔ Use graphical text to create a unique title for the top of each format.

Providing Content that Catches Your Audience's Attention

When using e-mail to promote products or services, your e-mails need to include descriptions and images that support your promotion. Here are some ideas and sources for creating promotional content to include in your e-mails:

✔ **Ask manufacturers for content.**

Companies that manufacture your products are great sources for product descriptions, images, and headlines.

✔ **Take digital photos.**

Use a digital camera to snap product photos and show your services in action.

✔ **Ask your customers for descriptions.**

Sometimes your customers can describe your products or services in ways that speak to your audience better than you can.

✔ **Ask people to write testimonials.**

Asking people to tell you about their experiences can be interesting and relevant to your audience. Shared experiences can also be powerful motivators for potential customers to make a purchase. Testimonials don't have to come from your customers. Sometimes you can find examples of other people who have used products and services like yours and demonstrate how their testimonial applies to your business.

Make sure you have permission to use testimonials.

✔ **Check your e-mail.**

Keeping track of the types of e-mails your customers and prospects send to you can give you insight into the topics that interest your audience. When your customers and prospects ask questions and make inquiries about your business, use your answers to develop content that promotes how your products or services help solve their problems. For example, a business consultant gets several e-mails asking about the impact of mobile marketing. She would be wise to create an e-mail addressing the most common questions related to mobile marketing as well as the services she provides.

Sending Valuable Offers

Although branding your e-mails and filling them with helpful information will catch your customer's attention, an offer may get your customer to act. *Offers* are conditional statements that give your audience one or more reasons to make an immediate decision instead of postponing a decision.

Offers don't necessarily have to require a purchase decision to have value. You can use offers just to motivate your audience to consider all the information about making a purchase decision. Whether your offers ask for an immediate purchase or just a visit to your Web site, they have to be valuable, or your audience won't act on them.

Because the value in postponing a decision almost always has to do with the fact that people prefer to hold on to their money, offers usually take the form of discounts and savings. Here are some of the most common e-mail offers:

- ✔ Coupons offering a discount

  Coupons contained in the body of your e-mail can be forwarded to anyone, so make sure you're ready to honor the unlimited use of your coupon by individuals who aren't on your e-mail list. If you want to make sure only select individuals use your coupon, you can ask your audience to request an official copy of the coupon; or, give every coupon a unique code and tell your audience that you will allow only one use per code.

- ✔ Incentives that reward a specific action (such as offering a membership to an exclusive automobile club upon purchase of a car)

- ✔ Giveaways of a complimentary product or service to one winner out of a limited number of participants who take a specific action

- ✔ Loss leaders that result in an immediate financial loss to your business but gain you a new customer who represents more profit in the future

- ✔ Urgent offers that fulfill a need that your audience perceives as an emergency, such as a sale on air conditioners during a heat wave

Writing an Effective Call to Action

Even when your content is valuable, most consumers simply scan and delete your e-mails unless you prompt them with alternatives. If you want to decrease your deletion rate, every e-mail you send needs to include a strong call to action. A *call to action* is a statement that prompts your audience to do something specific in favor of your objectives.

Calling your audience to action isn't as simple as including your phone number in the body of your e-mail or giving your audience lots of links to click. Consumers need directions and compelling reasons for taking specific actions, especially when their actions require spending time or money.

Anyone who reads e-mail is familiar with the stalwart phrase *Click Here*, but such generic phrases are not necessarily models for writing an effective call to action. An effective call to action is like a little sign that allows your audience to visualize the steps involved to take advantage of your e-mail's content, such as *Contact Us Today!*

Words are the building blocks of a strong call to action, and the quality and the number of words you choose significantly affects how many responses you receive. The most effective way to write a call to action is to begin with *action* words: verbs that propose a specific task to your audience.

Following are calls to action, paired with strong verbs to help motivate a reader to act. If you want your audience to take a certain action, try working these action-word suggestions into your e-mail:

- **Read your e-mail:** Read, look, consider, notice, scroll

- **Fill out a form:** Contact, respond, comment, advise

- **Save your e-mail:** Save, keep, store, file, move

- **Request information:** Download, request, learn, e-mail, compare

- ✔ **Print your e-mail:** Print, post, bring, hang
- ✔ **Visit a physical location:** Drive, come, park, attend
- ✔ **Forward your e-mail:** Forward, share, send, refer
- ✔ **Visit a Web page:** Visit, view, go, navigate
- ✔ **Make a purchase:** Buy, add, purchase, own, order
- ✔ **Register for an event:** Register, reserve, sign up, R.S.V.P.
- ✔ **Phone your business:** Call, phone, dial
- ✔ **Make an appointment:** Schedule, arrange, meet, set up

Here's how you can build on action words to create a strong call to action. You can see the progression of the call to action as you make it stronger and stronger:

1. **Combine your action word with the subject of the action word.**

   Order *this item.*

2. **Include the place where the action happens.**

   Order this item *online.*

3. **Add the urgency of the action.**

   Order this item online *before Friday.*

4. **Finish with an adjective to underscore the value inherent in the action.**

   Order this *hilarious* item online before Friday.

The combination of one or more action words along with your supplementary words makes a complete call to action. Writing an effective call to action can be more of an art than a science, but becoming a good call to action writer is just a matter of practice.

Turning your action words into links is a great way to prompt your audience to click to take action.

Understanding Basic E-Mail Tracking Data

One of the most practical and valuable features of using e-mail to market your business is using e-mail tracking reports to find out what your audience is doing with your e-mails after you send them.

You have to be an advanced HTML and database programmer to track e-mails on your own, but an e-mail service provider (ESP) can track your e-mails for you. ESPs automatically add a special tracking code to the links you include in your e-mails. The tracking code is unique to each individual on your e-mail list and is tied to each e-mail campaign. ESPs also have programs that automatically read the code from other e-mail servers when they return undeliverable messages, so you don't have to do the hard work to determine why a particular e-mail wasn't delivered.

E-mail tracking reports are analytical summaries of the results of a given e-mail campaign that can tell you

- Which e-mails bounced
- Why they bounced
- Who opened your e-mails
- What links they clicked
- Who unsubscribed from your e-mails
- Who forwarded your e-mails

Analyzing the data from your tracking report will let you know if you need to refine your e-mail marketing strategy.

Chapter 5

Social Media Marketing

Social media is a buzzphrase that describes a wide array of conversational tools on the Internet. These tools help Web users connect, converse, and make better use of the resources they find online.

Today, social media is a complex web of sites and software that allows you to bookmark, discuss, vent, and then share with other people. Social media users represent an enormous market. Facebook alone has over 500 million active users. That number is according to Facebook, but hey! — even if it's exaggerated and you divide that number in half, it's still a lot of people.

You need to understand this space of social media. You can reach out to customers, find new audiences, and talk to existing ones in more ways than ever. Even if you're not doing any social media marketing, your customers are there, talking about you. Knowing where they talk and how to answer them is critical.

This chapter explains social media; separates truth from fiction; and then demonstrates specific business strategies for major social media outlets, such as Facebook, LinkedIn, and YouTube.

Marketing, Social Media Style

Social media sites and tools enable you to build your reputation and audience over time. Every friend you add on Facebook, every bookmark you add to StumbleUpon, and every post you make on a microblog increases your profile.

If you spend this capital wisely, you can use it to

- Announce a new product.

- Ask everyone for feedback about a new idea or blog post.

- Build some buzz and get others talking about you — and your online presence.

Why social media is so important: The sneeze principle

Here's one critical lesson of social media: the *sneeze principle.* Any social media allows a visitor to watch a video, read an article, or see some other content. Then it lets the visitor *sneeze:* That is, a visitor can somehow indicate he agrees (or disagrees) with that content by leaving a comment, posting a bookmark, checking an I'm a Fan check box, or doing something else.

That's the sneeze effect: When that first visitor sneezes, others see it. They go and look at the same content. Then they might sneeze, too. So *their* circle of friends sees the same thing, and has the option of transmitting the message even further.

Here's an example:

Joe reads a funny blog post and gives it a thumbs-up on StumbleUpon. Joe also has about 50 fans on StumbleUpon, and they all see that he liked that post. They go and read it, too. A few of them really like it, so they give it a thumbs-up. They each have 40–400 fans, who then see that someone they follow liked the post. In a matter of hours, this one blog post has been sneezed to thousands of visitors.

It's not as easy as it sounds, but if you understand the sneeze principle, you understand why social media can be so powerful.

The catch? If the networks or their members think you're using them to promote yourself, they'll penalize you or ban you altogether.

The remainder of this chapter is dedicated to dealing with walking that fine line between market research and promotion and self-aggrandizement to help you learn your way around — and exploit — this diverse and expanding marketing medium.

Exploring Social Media

Social media umbrellas any Web site or Web application that allows your audience to interact with your site and each other, directly or indirectly. Table 5-1 shows the seven basic categories of social media sites.

Table 5-1	Social Media Sites by Category	
Social Media Type	*Description*	*Examples*
Blogs	Allow you to write, journal-style, and then invite comments from your readers	Blogger WordPress
Social networks	Where people can interact and connect online	Facebook MySpace PartnerUp
Bookmarking sites	Allow you to save bookmarks, just like you would in your browser, but on a site you can access from any computer	Delicious Gnolia StumbleUpon
Microblogging sites	Allow you to blog one or two sentences at a time	Twitter Plurk
Media sharing sites	Where you can upload and share video, audio, and photographs	YouTube Flickr
Popularity sites	Where you can collect bookmarks and then let visitors vote on them	Digg Reddit
Aggregators	Help the truly social and connected keep up with all this stuff	FriendFeed

---

Beware of social network spam

Social network operators do not like spammers! Don't use a social network to make friends with hundreds of strangers and then start sending them coupons or other offers. Chances are you'll end up getting kicked off the network. Instead, approach them like you would at a party. Say hello. Shake hands. Chat a bit. Make your sales pitch only when someone states he's looking for the product or service you provide.

All seven categories are important for you to explore because they're all interconnected: A Facebook member may also have a YouTube account. If someone forwards her a funny video via Facebook, she can zip over to YouTube to watch it. Then, she might tell her Facebook friends. If one of those friends has a Twitter account and posts, his 540 Twitter friends might see it, too.

Social media, more than any other vehicle, has the potential to spread a message far and fast.

You also need to know what sites are social media hot spots and what each site's specialty is so you can successfully use social media to spread the word about your products or services online.

The following sections look at social networks and microblogging, two of the most powerful tools in your social media arsenal.

Connecting via social networks

Social networks are sites that let you create your own profile, seek out and connect with other members, and talk to your friends from a single profile page. Social networks also let you share photos, images, links, and other tidbits of information within your circle of friends.

Facebook, MySpace, and hundreds (if not thousands) of other sites all qualify as social networks.

At their simplest, these networks offer you — and your online presence — a great opportunity to

- **Get a feel for your potential customers.** Social networks help you find friends and users by interests, geography, and hobbies.

- **Get advice from colleagues.** Services like LinkedIn offer special Answers networks where you can ask and answer questions from other members.

- **Demonstrate your expertise.** You can tell your social network friends about recent accomplishments, answer their questions, and provide the occasional tip.

After you start using the more advanced features on the major social networks, you can also

- **Distribute custom tools** by using these networks' special development kits.

- **Create targeted discussion groups** by using features like Facebook Groups.

Here is a list of social networks that you should be familiar with. They've been around for a while, have thousands or millions of users, and offer access to the widest audience:

- **Facebook:** One of the dominant sites, Facebook (`www.facebook.com`) allows you to create your own profile pages. You can send messages to other members and make friends by adding fellow members to your Friends lists. Facebook also allows custom applications: games, puzzles, utilities, and other little widgets created by third-party developers. You can join for free by creating an account in just a few minutes.

- **MySpace:** Waning in popularity but still dominant, MySpace (`www.myspace.com`) predates Facebook, offering much of the same toolset and features. The site also allows custom *skins* (designs) for your profile page and has served as a launchpad for up-and-coming performers. As with Facebook, you can join MySpace for free in just a few minutes.

- **LinkedIn:** A network for businesspeople, LinkedIn (`www.linkedin.com`) is business networking on steroids. After you create a detailed profile, businesspeople worldwide can connect with you based on common interests, previous work together, or networking groups. Members can create networks of literally hundreds of people. Although joining LinkedIn is free, some features are only available for a fee.

- **Yahoo! Answers:** Have a question? Visit `http://answers.yahoo.com`. Thousands of helpful members offer answers to questions on topics ranging from Internet marketing to wedding planning to pet care. Joining is free and answering questions is easy. Plus you get a nice ego boost when someone picks your answer as best.

- **Discussion forums:** Forums are still out there. Sites like PartnerUp.com (`www.partnerup.com`) and Score Community (`www.scorecommunity.org`) are basically enormous collections of discussion threads where you create your membership and then join the fray. Most discussion forums are free to join.

All social networking sites offer a rare opportunity to spread the word about yourself or your company to thousands, or even millions, of people. The trick is doing it politely.

Microblogging

Microblog sites allow members to make lots of short blog posts. And by *short,* we mean **short** — often less than 140 characters. Microblogs are fast, easy, and can be updated from a cellphone, computer, or even via voice mail.

Microblogs look and feel more like old-fashioned chat rooms than blogs. Participants post statements, which are visible in a common public timeline, which everyone can see and read.

You might think that microblogging is just like a social network, but microblogs tend to be more "real time," with some participants posting every few minutes. So they allow for more of an ongoing conversation. But yes, the lines do get blurry at times.

Microbloggers can follow fellow participants whom they find interesting. After you make friends on a microblog, you follow them, and they follow you. Then their friends see you and follow you, and so on. On most microblogs, you mark people as friends by clicking Friend, or Follow. Then they confirm, and you're friends. It's that easy.

So microblogging is a great way to build a focused audience to which you can pose questions, make suggestions, or announce a new blog post.

Of the few microblogs out there, Twitter (`http://twitter.com`) is by far the most prominent. Half addiction, half publicity platform, Twitter is a microblogging tool with which you can enter 140-character messages. By following other people you find interesting, you'll receive their messages. Think of it as a huge chat room that remembers what you said. Joining is free. Like most social networks, you create a simple identity and can start posting right away.

Twitter allows you to see the most recent posts on the network and statistics regarding who's following you. When you post, your followers' Twitter timeline automatically updates to show your post. If you announce a new blog post, for example, many of them will read it right away.

Researching Your Audience

Social media is unique enough that you'll want to analyze your audience there, separately from other vehicles, such as search engines. For example, you might expect instant sales from a paid search ad or an e-mail marketing campaign. But when it comes to social media, you're looking for evidence of steady inroads with your audience, such as increased blog mentions about your company, which won't lead to sales for weeks or months.

Asking the right questions

When you research your audience, you need to answer five basic questions:

- ✔ **What kinds of people are in your audience?** You need to know whom you're speaking to.

- ✔ **Why are they participating in the community?** What do they want from it? If they're participating so they can trade pictures of their pet bunny rabbit with friends, and you suddenly show up selling hunting rifles, they won't appreciate it.

- ✔ **What communities and sites do they most often use?** Focus your efforts where your audience goes.

- ✔ **How big is this audience?** If a social media campaign on Facebook is going to reach 20 people in six months, for example, Facebook might not be your ideal venue.

- ✔ **How often do they participate?** This, combined with audience size, helps you determine how often you need to participate. It lets you be more efficient.

Write all five questions down so that you can take notes in a worksheet while you research.

The worksheet is your central storage for research, so keep it handy.

Starting with online communities

To answer the five questions posed in the previous section, spend some time exploring a few communities to see what your potential audience is saying and doing. Take a look at the following sites:

- ✔ **Google Groups:** Visit `www.partnerup.com`. Search for your product or service and then look around some of the discussions that you find. What are people asking? See whether you could contribute to the discussion. How active are the discussions? If participants are posting every hour, this is a very active community — you'll need to follow closely if you're going to participate. Make sure you're receiving updates via e-mail so that you can respond quickly.

- ✔ **Yahoo! Groups:** Search and review Yahoo! Groups (`http://groups.yahoo.com/`) for the same kinds of information as Google Groups.

- ✔ **Facebook:** `Facebook.com` is so big, and so busy, that groups exist for nearly every imaginable interest. Search Facebook Groups for the topics that relate to your business. See how many members these groups have: More members mean a bigger audience for you. And don't forget to look at how often participants post to groups, because frequent posts mean a more active community.

- ✔ **Digg:** Search `Digg.com` for topics, products, people, or ideas related to your business. If people are submitting relevant stories, how are they received? If relevant stories get a lot of votes, you have an interested community of readers, and social news sites are a potential venue for you. If relevant stories are received with sarcastic comments and a handful of votes, you'll want to avoid social news sites — or find a different way to approach the topic. The now-famous Will it Blend? YouTube videos are a great example of this: Blenders don't make good Digg material. But shoving an iPod into a blender? Pure Digg gold!

- ✔ **Blogs:** Use Google Blog Search (`http://blogsearch.google.com`), `Technorati.com`, and `Icerocket.com`. Search again for topics relevant to your business. How many bloggers are writing about the topic? The more bloggers, and the more often they're posting, the larger and potentially receptive your audience. What do the bloggers focus on? Their interests may indicate your audience's interests, too.

Audience research is the most important research you can do. Data is great, but social media marketing is not easily quantified — the general feel you get by checking out the communities is essential, too.

When you look at each community, note what you find on your social media research worksheet.

Branding and Publicity: Facebook Pages and Facebook Events

Facebook is the current social networking leader. With tens of millions of users, Facebook offers an audience for nearly any business.

You may already be familiar with Facebook profiles (you might have a personal profile already) and groups (chances are good if you have a profile, you've already joined a group . . . or ten), but Facebook offers two other kinds of community builders: Pages and Events.

Think of Facebook Pages as trade show booths, and Events as invitations handed out to everyone. You can use the two to announce new products or services, solicit questions from your loyal customers, or provide special incentives.

Building a company presence with Pages

The primary branding and publicity tool on Facebook (if you don't want to spend money) is *Facebook Pages* (`http://www.facebook.com/pages/`). Don't confuse these with a standard profile page. Facebook Pages provides a customizable page where you can add your own Flash animations, Facebook applications, images, and text.

If visitors like the page, they can click the Like button. When visitors do that, their friends will see it, and then go and look at the page, too. And so on.

Here's how to create a great Facebook Page:

- ✔ **Develop an idea that's more than advertising.** Don't just create a billboard. Design a page that teaches visitors something new every day, offers them access to a special tool, or entertains them.

- ✔ **Write well.** If you're not a professional copywriter, hiring one is worth it. You don't have much time to convince the visitor that they should stay and Like the page.

- ✔ **Have great graphics.** If you don't have professional-looking illustrations or photos, don't use any at all.

- ✔ **Make the page "sneezable."** Use photos and short, punchy messages that visitors can quickly scan, read, and pass along. (Read about the sneeze principle in the sidebar, "Why social media is so important: The sneeze principle," earlier in this chapter.)

- ✔ **Update it!**

Announcing cool stuff with Facebook Events

Facebook Events is another great publicity tool. When you create an event, you can invite any of your Facebook friends, as well as non-Facebook members.

Facebook Events is a great tool *if you don't abuse it.* However, the more events you announce, the less folks will read them. Be sure to read the rules for Facebook Events, too.

Use Facebook Events if

- ✔ **You have a specific event you want to promote.** The event can be online or at a real location, or just be a silly made-up occasion that you think might be fun.

- ✔ **You want to build some buzz around that event.**

- ✔ **You have specific people on Facebook you want to invite or otherwise inform about the event.**

Here are four things to always include on a Facebook Events page:

- ✔ **A great event name:** Using something akin to "Tour Our Store" is fine, but using "Store Sale & Tour at Widgets R Us" might garner more interest.

- ✔ **A great image:** Again, a great graphic will go a long way toward making folks stick around and read about your event.

- ✔ **A great guest list:** If you can get some well-known folks on the guest list *and* have a public guest list so folks can see it, others are more likely to sign up. Same goes for the number of guests. Social proof is very compelling.

- ✔ **Updates:** And yes, once again, periodic updates are essential. Don't forget about the event page after you're done. Post photos, videos, and notes about the event. Then you can use that page to boost your next event by saying, "Look at how much fun the last event was."

Networking for Business on LinkedIn

LinkedIn is an entirely different kind of social network. Built entirely as a vehicle with which businesspeople connect and interact, it functions based on connections rather than friends. Although this might sound like a purely semantic difference, it's not, and here's why:

- ✔ **LinkedIn restricts whom you can add as a connection.** You need to be able to indicate how you know that person before you can even attempt to connect.

- ✔ **LinkedIn includes recommendations that you can get from colleagues and clients.** Those recommendations show on your profile page.

- ✔ **Your profile includes your work history.**

- ✔ **People are automatically grouped by company.**

- ✔ **You can't contact people who aren't in your network directly except through InMail,** for which LinkedIn charges a fee.

- ✔ **Companies can get their own separate profile pages** (a new feature).

Use LinkedIn if

- ✔ Your company provides professional services.

- ✔ Your clients are other companies.

- ✔ You're a consultant of almost any kind.

- ✔ You want to focus on quality connections, not quantity.

You can't customize the look and feel of your profile page on LinkedIn. However, completeness is important — even more important than on Facebook and MySpace — because LinkedIn is driven by one-to-one connections between individuals, and those connections are typically formed based on work history, location, and so on. It's a pure business networking environment.

To give yourself the best chance of succeeding on LinkedIn, heed these four things:

- ✔ **Quality:** A few quality connections will take you a lot farther than dozens of lousy ones. Connect with folks you already know, or have someone else introduce you using the introduction feature on LinkedIn.

- ✔ **Recommendations:** Get recommendations when you can. They look great on your profile page, and many potential clients will research you via LinkedIn.

- ✔ **Groups:** The LinkedIn groups feature works much like MySpace and Facebook, but LinkedIn groups focus entirely on professional networking.

- ✔ **Answers:** Use LinkedIn Answers to provide or seek advice. If you provide great information, folks will mark your answer as "best." Get enough of those, and you'll be tagged as having expertise in a particular subject.

LinkedIn is a very specialized network. Don't go in there expecting to sell 400 insurance policies. Set up your profile with the expectation that you can make valuable, long-lasting business connections.

Spreading the Word on YouTube

A popular video on YouTube (www.youtube.com/) can get tens of thousands of views (or even hundreds of thousands). But, as you've likely figured out by now, getting a big hit on any social network, YouTube included, takes a lot of work.

Use YouTube if you

- Have pre-existing video content, and all you have to do is upload it
- Have entertainment-based content
- Want to introduce a wide audience to training, branding, or other videos
- Are going to produce a series of short videos

YouTube has a few rules you should know about, too:

- Videos must be ten minutes or shorter.
- Videos must meet YouTube's file-size guidelines, which vary depending on the file format.
- You must have permission to publish the video on YouTube!

Here are some tips for YouTube success:

- **Keep it short.** The most successful videos on YouTube are two to three minutes long. Obviously, if you're doing a training piece, your video might have to be longer, but try to create a series of short videos instead, if you can.

- ✔ **Make friends.** You can easily forget YouTube is a social network and just start uploading videos. Find folks who create great content, make friends with them, and comment on their videos. They'll reciprocate.

- ✔ **Complete your profile.** Just like on any other social network, a complete profile will establish trust when other users come looking.

- ✔ **Respond to comments!** If someone comments on your video, reply. Say, "Thanks" or "Good point" or whatever's relevant. It's called *social* media for a reason.

- ✔ **Write a good title for your video.** The title is what gets folks to watch. *My Road Trip* isn't as good as *Pulled Over In Louisiana.*

- ✔ **Write a good description.** A keyword-rich description increases your chance of a good ranking in Google's blended search results.

- ✔ **When you post a new video, tell your friends.** YouTube partly ranks videos according to the number of views and view *velocity* (the rate at which you're getting those views). If you can get a little mob watching the video, it'll give you a boost.

Obeying the (Unspoken) Rules

Social media can be a great way to market your business — provided you don't ruffle any feathers in the community. Here are a few of the unspoken social media rules that will help you stay on people's good sides:

Crass promotion is never okay

If you find yourself writing something like "10% off sale on my site! Come now!" then pinch yourself and delete your post. This kind of thing will only alienate your friends. It might even lead to penalties from the Web site owners.

Promoting yourself is okay. Just keep it a bit lower-key. Something like the following is generally acceptable:

Shameless plug: I just published a new book about Internet marketing. Please have a look at www.mybookwebsite.com.

The following is not acceptable, especially if you repeat it ten times per day:

Buy my new book! Learn how to earn millions online! www. mybooksite.com.

Don't post angry

No one can follow this rule 100 percent of the time. Eventually, someone will say something that really makes you angry, and you'll retort and click Submit before you can stop yourself.

If you snap back at someone, *everyone sees it.* It can reflect on you, your company, and your entire online identity.

So whenever possible, avoid the angry post. If you're inexorably drawn into an online shouting match, try these strategies:

- **Take 5. Take 10. Take 100.** Turn off the computer. Go outside. You'll be surprised how minor the offending post or comment seems later.

- **Go to the source.** Contact the person via private or direct message. Instead of a slap fight, try asking, "Hey, did I just misunderstand?" or "What'd I do?"

- **Vent in private.** Get it out of your system by first writing an angry reply in a word processor. Then step back, take a breath, and edit it to be more diplomatic. Only then, post it.

Do apologize

No matter what you do, at some point, you're going to shove your foot firmly into your mouth. Social media is still *social* — you're often talking to people all over the planet, and misunderstandings happen. If you offend, overreact, or just forget about a request someone made, just let him know you're sorry.

Social media is all about online karma: The community will generally remember how you behave, but no one expects perfection. A little humility goes a long way.

Do be a good citizen

Help others if they have questions about how to use the site or network. Lend a hand, just as others probably helped you when you signed up.

Do add value

Contribute to the community. If you're microblogging, contributing can be as simple as posting an interesting link or video. On social networks, support the groups to which you belong by answering questions and inviting others to join.

You don't have to be the top expert in your field to add value. Value can mean humor, a sympathetic ear, an interesting link, or just pointing a few people in the right direction.

Chapter 6

Ten Tips for Effective Online Marketing

*D*elving into an online marketing campaign can be a bit intimidating. You don't want to unwittingly offend any potential customers by breaking one of the Internet's many unwritten rules. And how can you ensure that you're making the most of your marketing budget? Read on and relax; with these helpful tips, your campaign will go swimmingly.

Don't Yell at Your Visitors

When using text on your Web site or e-mail, don't capitalize everything in a sentence. You may want to share your excitement about a great sale you're having, but writing in all caps is the equivalent of shouting at the top of your lungs.

Practice "White Hat" SEO Tactics

When it comes to search engine optimization (SEO) strategies, two approaches exist:

- **Black hat SEO** uses tactics specifically designed to improve search rankings and fool the search engines into providing a higher ranking than a Web site should actually receive according to that search engine's algorithms.
- **White hat SEO** uses tactics to make a Web site as acceptable as possible to both visitors and search engines, without attempting to manipulate the search engines.

Strictly speaking, no ethical reason exists not to use black hat SEO tactics to try for a higher ranking. However, this is a lousy business plan. Assuming that your business plan allows for growth over a period of years, it pays to practice white hat SEO tactics — rely on content and natural link growth, with a little help here and there — rather than tricks.

Balance Competition Against Search Volume

Some terms might be so relevant and offer so many potential visitors that any level of competition is worth it. For example, the phrase *wedding dresses* gets over one million searches per month. It's also one of the most competitive phrases on the Internet. But one million searches makes *wedding dresses* so potentially valuable that, if you have any chance of gaining a front-page ranking for it, you have to try. Sometimes, braving the competition is worth it, because the traffic is so rich.

Make the Most of Your Products and Services

Look at every product or service you offer. If you can break them up into smaller sub-products or services, do it, and write about each of those. For example, *bicycle repair* can be broken up into *tune ups*, *wheel truing*, *frame repair*, and *painting*. *Accounting* can be divided into *tax*, *bookkeeping*, and *cash flow*. The more terms you provide, the greater the chances that someone searching for your services or products will find you.

Keep Your PPC Keyword List Concise

The fewer keywords you use in an ad group, the better. A good rule is to have no more than 30 keywords in an ad group. A keyword list of several hundred terms is hard to manage and affects both the ad group and the campaign in many negative ways, including relevancy, quality score, ease of ad-text creation, and bidding.

The more targeted and more specific your ad group is, the more benefits you reap from search engines in terms of PPC, relevancy, and ad position.

Choose Keywords with a Proven Track Record

Google has a free site that's dedicated to tracking trends on keywords over time. On the Google Insights for Search site (`www.google.com/insights/search`), you can enter a keyword and see how many searches were made on it as far back as 2004. You can filter searches by location worldwide and by time ranges, as well as compare keywords.

Keep a Separate Media E-Mail List

Most media entities accept press releases via e-mail and will post additional e-mail addresses for communicating newsworthy information person to person. If you're planning to send press releases, be sure to keep your media list separate from your customer list so that you can restrict media personnel to newsworthy press release e-mails only.

Permission, privacy, and professionalism matter just as much to the media as they do to the consumer. So kindly contact your media professionals and ask them to be on your press release list before you start sending.

Make Sure Your Audience Knows Your E-Mails Are from You

Because the people in your audience likely receive many e-mails a day, you need to ensure that they know who has sent your e-mail — otherwise, it might just end up being deleted. Ask yourself how your audience is most likely to recognize you, and craft your From line to include that information.

Keep a Virtual Presence at Your Real-World Events

If you're hosting an event at a physical location and you've promoted it via a Facebook Event, try to have a laptop and an Internet connection onsite. Posting an occasional note, photo, or video might create an impromptu audience on Facebook.

Build a Twitter Following

To make microblogs such as Twitter worth your while, you need to accumulate a lot of followers. Then you can capitalize on that to launch a new product, blog post, or site if you follow a few basic steps:

- ✔ **Set up a complete profile.** The more detail, the more easily others can decide whether they want to keep in touch.

- ✔ **Follow others.** Look around. Who are some of the biggest participants in the community? Follow them by clicking Follow or the similar button in their profile. They'll likely follow you, too, at some point.

- ✔ **Announce that you joined.** If you have a blog, let everyone know you just joined the microblog and provide your account name. Existing members who see that will probably follow you, too.

- ✔ **Contribute.** If you find an interesting link, have a bit of trivia, or just a funny observation, post it! Microblogs are very informal. If you own a smartphone or your cellphone has a Web browser, set up mobile access as well.

- ✔ **Reply.** If someone you're following posts something that catches your attention, let him know.

- ✔ **Be consistent.** Set a goal for a number of daily microblog posts, and stick to it. If you fall silent on Twitter, your followers may abandon you.

Grow your business online with Deluxe.

- Help your customers find your business. Get online!
- Our helpful 24/7 customer support will assist you.
- Web design and hosting.
- Domain names and enhanced search results.
- Professional copywriting.
- Deluxe hosts more than 400,000 websites.
- Services provided by Aplus.net,® a Deluxe company.

Additional Deluxe resources:

Small Business Blog
deluxesmallbizblog.com

Small Business Community
partnerup.com

Free Marketing Assessment
marketstronger.com

Free Marketing Webinars
deluxe.com/webinars

Find us on Facebook
facebook.com/deluxecorp

Follow us on Twitter
twitter.com/deluxecorp